A Volunteer Helps

by Timothy Prentiss

Table of Contents

collect

donated

help

job

What Is a Volunteer?

A volunteer works to help others. Volunteers do not earn money for their work.

▲ These volunteers help collect food for the hungry.

A volunteer has an important
job. A volunteer works to help
others. Sometimes volunteers work
to help the environment. Volunteers
work hard at their jobs.

▲ These volunteers plant trees for the future.

How Do Volunteers Help?

A volunteer helps in many ways. For example, a volunteer can help serve lunches to others.

▲ These volunteers are working. Many hungry people will get good meals.

Do you like to share your time?
Do you like to read? A volunteer
can read to others.

▲ Students who like to
read can be volunteers.

How Can You Be a Volunteer?

Do you like to help? You can be a volunteer! What kind of volunteer will you be?

▲ Do you love animals? Then you can be a volunteer.

Think about what you like to do. Do you like to build things? You can build things and be a volunteer at the same time.

▲ These volunteers help to build a house for people who cannot afford a home.

How Can Volunteers Help at School?

Your school needs many volunteers. You can be a volunteer in your classroom. You can help your teacher.

▲ These volunteers care for the class pet.

Some volunteers help after school. These boys like to be outside. They are going to a park. The boys will help clean up the park.

▲ These boys are excited to help.

Some jobs are big. Volunteers can work with others. A job gets done faster when volunteers work together.

▲ These volunteers pick up trash near the school.

You can help clean your school.

▲ These volunteers race to see who can clean the fastest.

Do You Know a Volunteer?

Who are volunteers that you know?
Ask volunteers what they do. Tell them
what you like to do. Can they help
you be a volunteer, too?

▲ Volunteers can collect toys
that people have donated.

▲ Volunteers can collect trash at the beach.

Look around you. Do you see people who need help? You can be a volunteer. Your job will be important!